Seamless Patterns

Adult Coloring Books
Stress Relieving Patterns

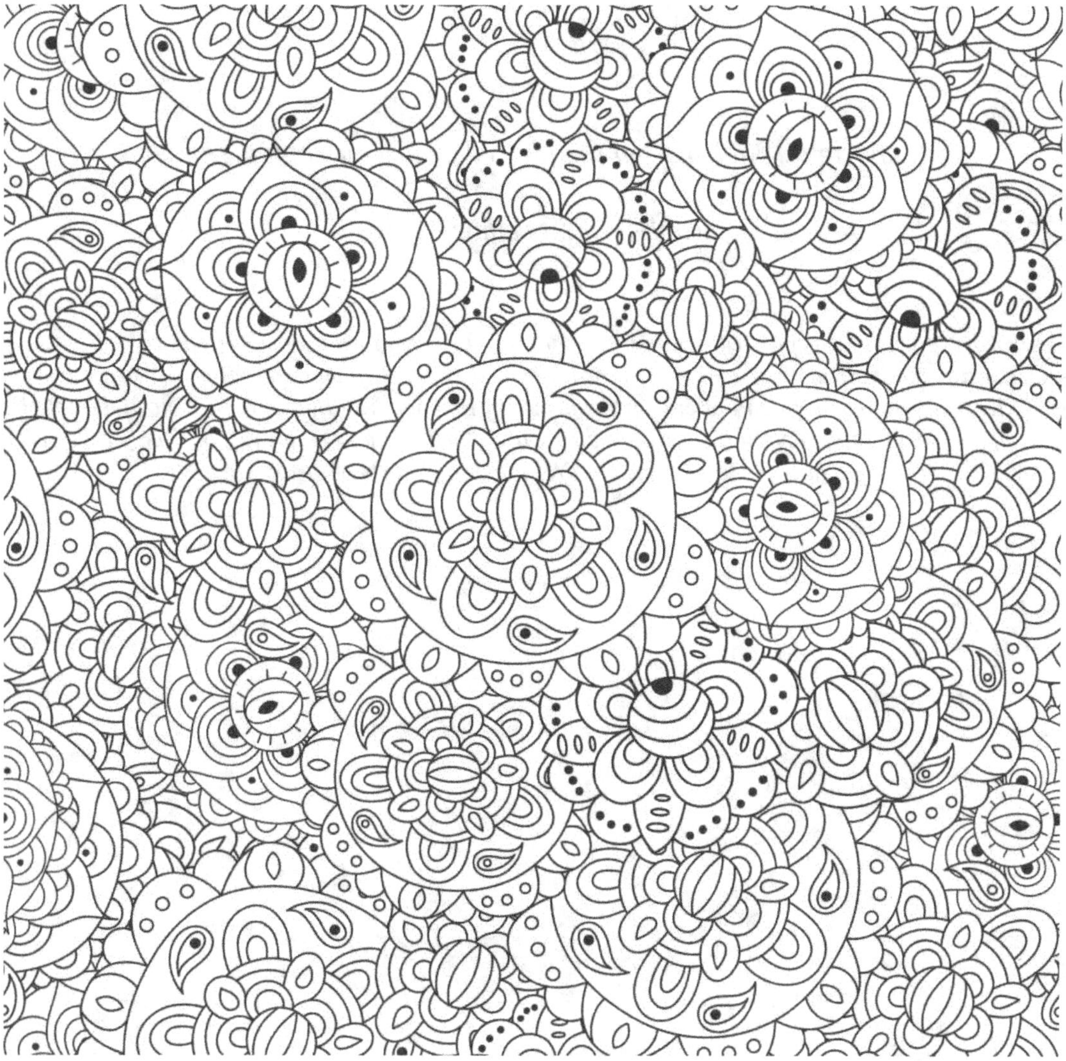

Sophia Payne

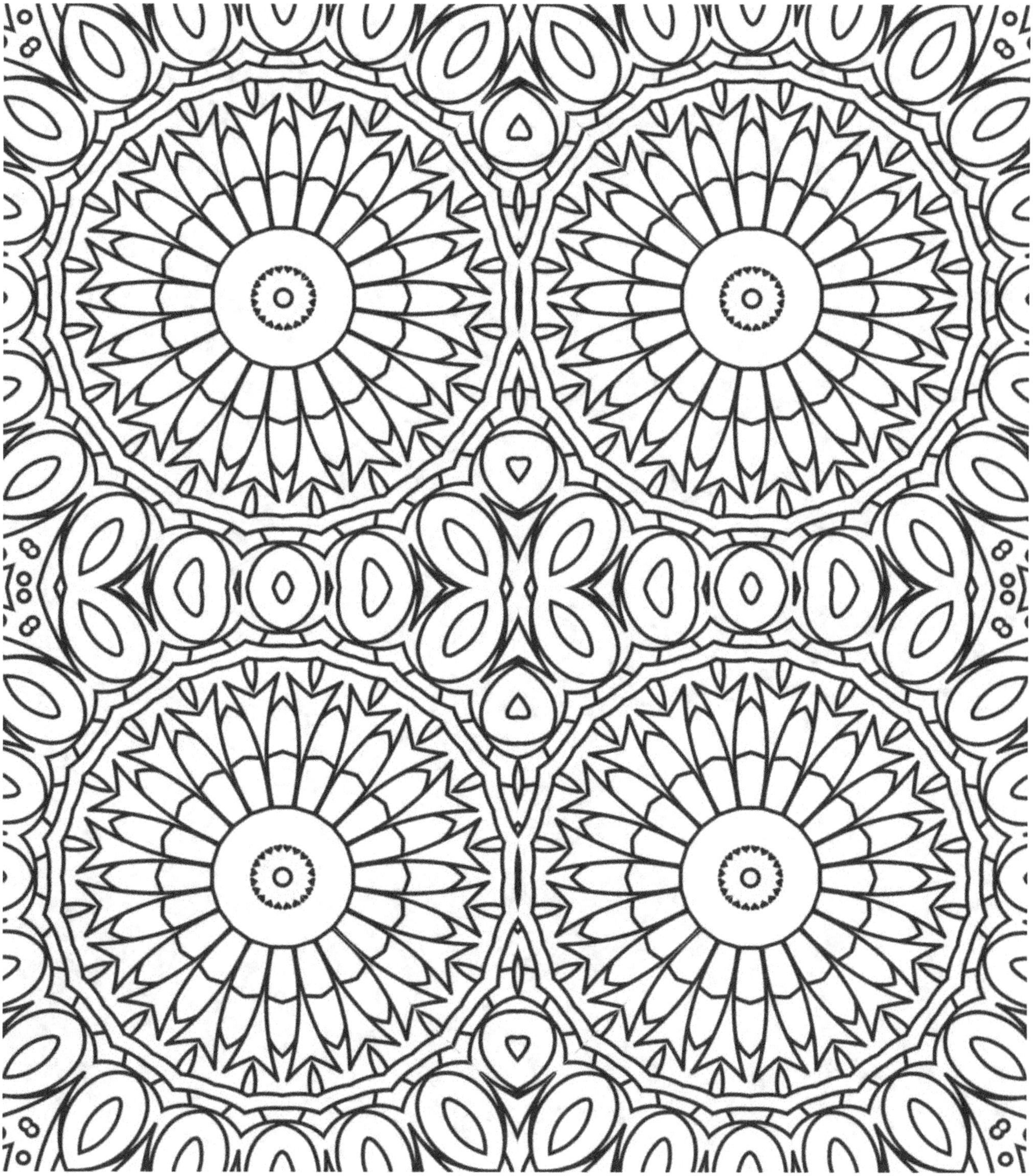

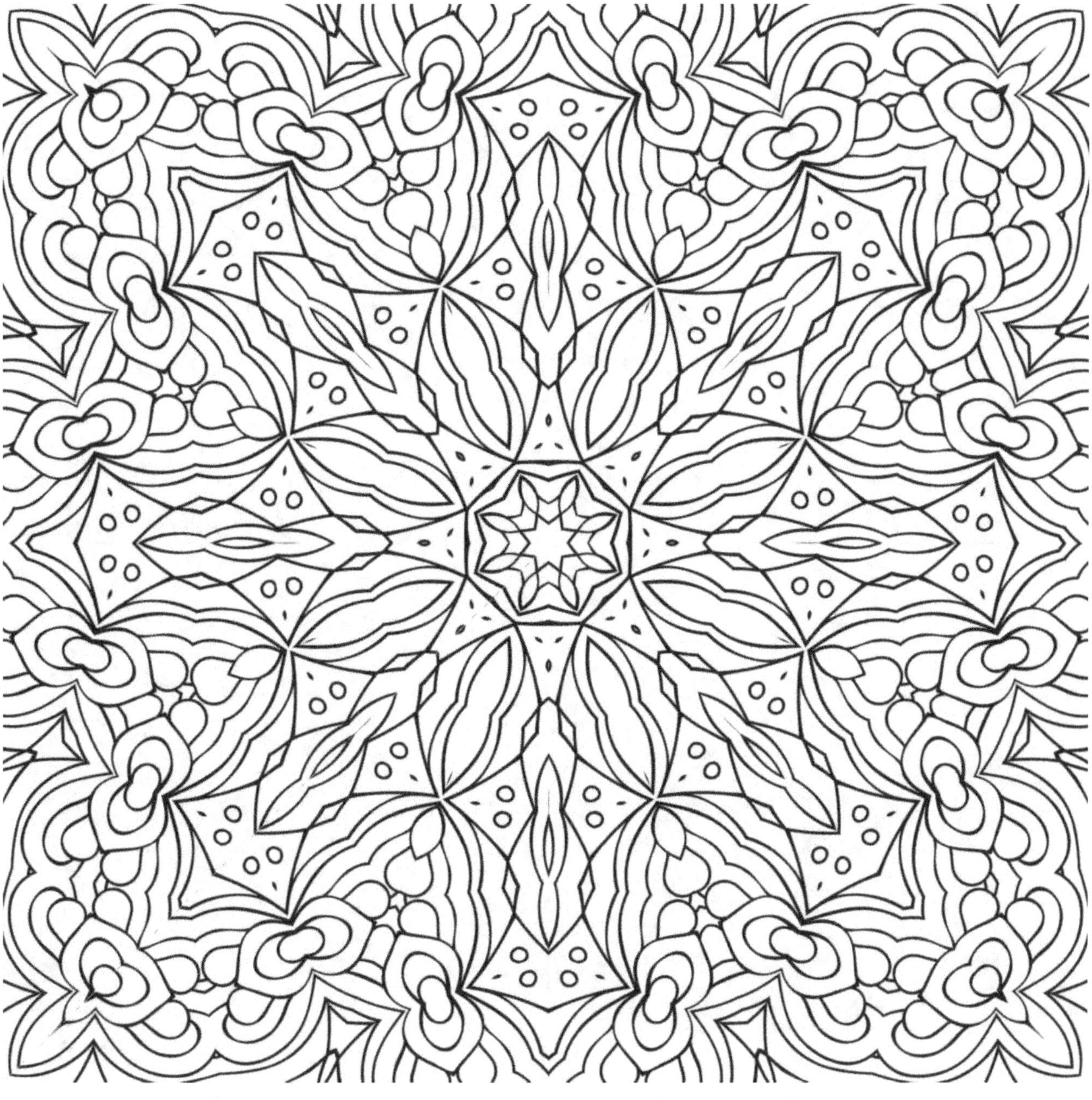

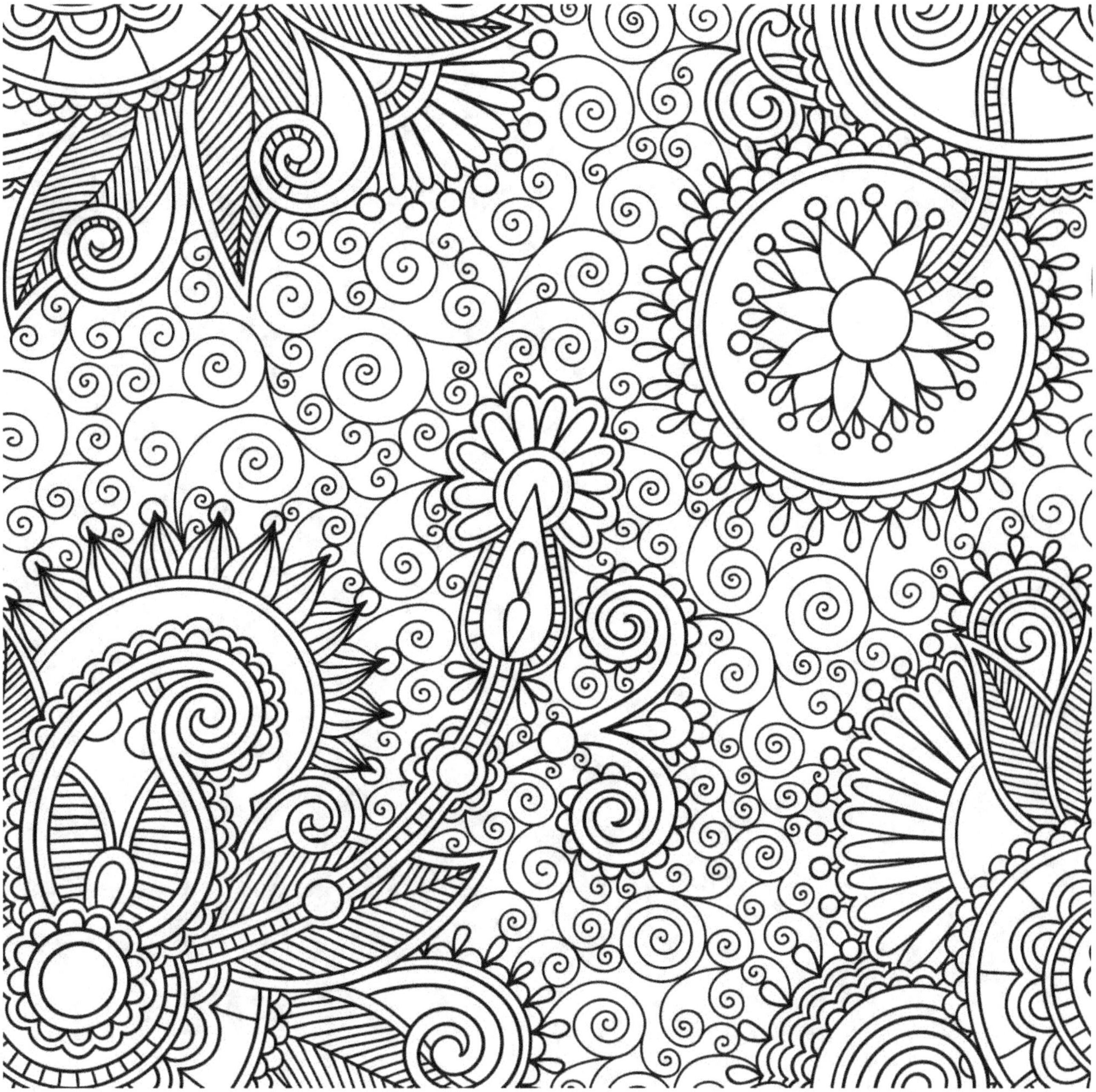

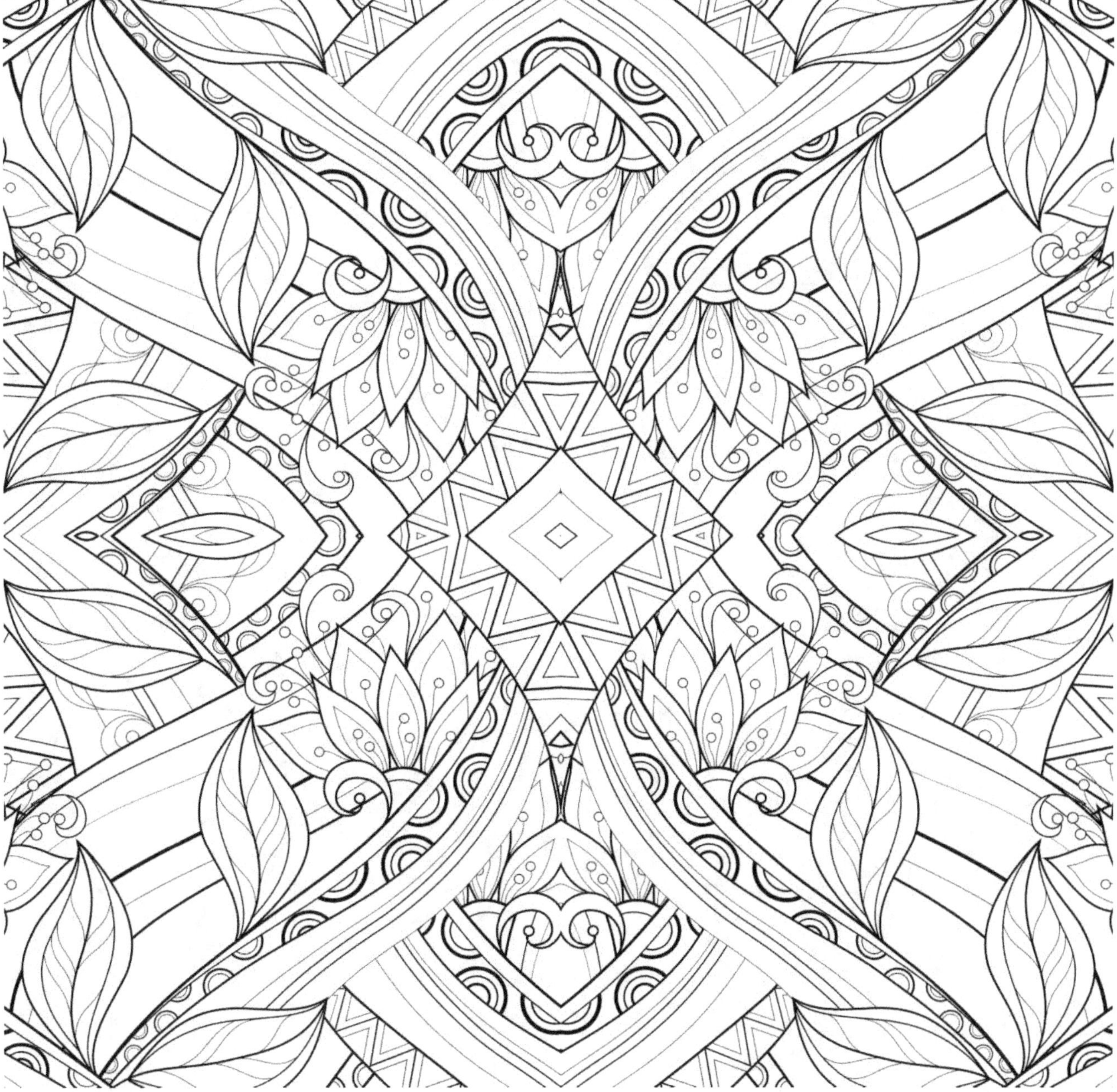

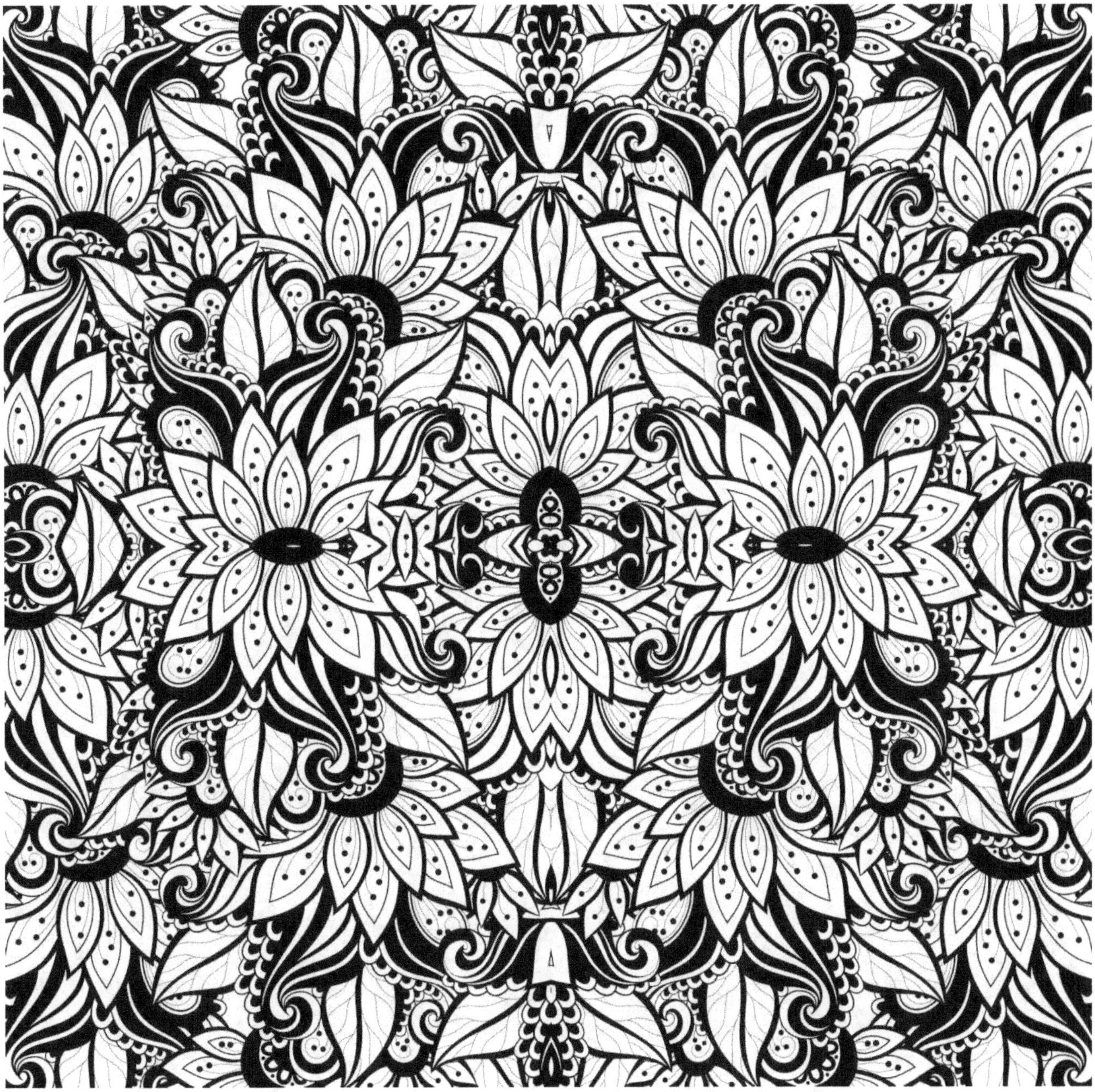

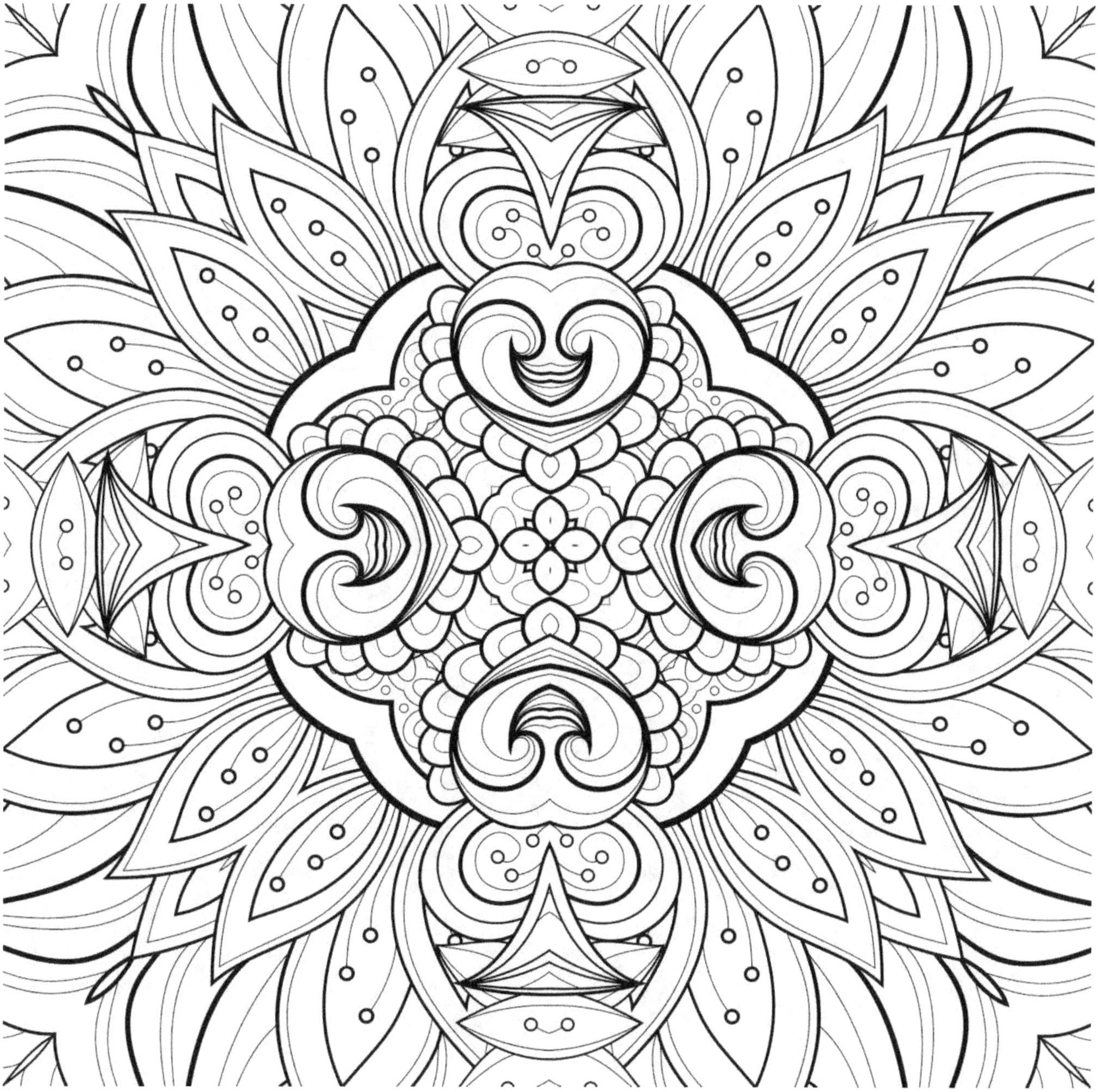

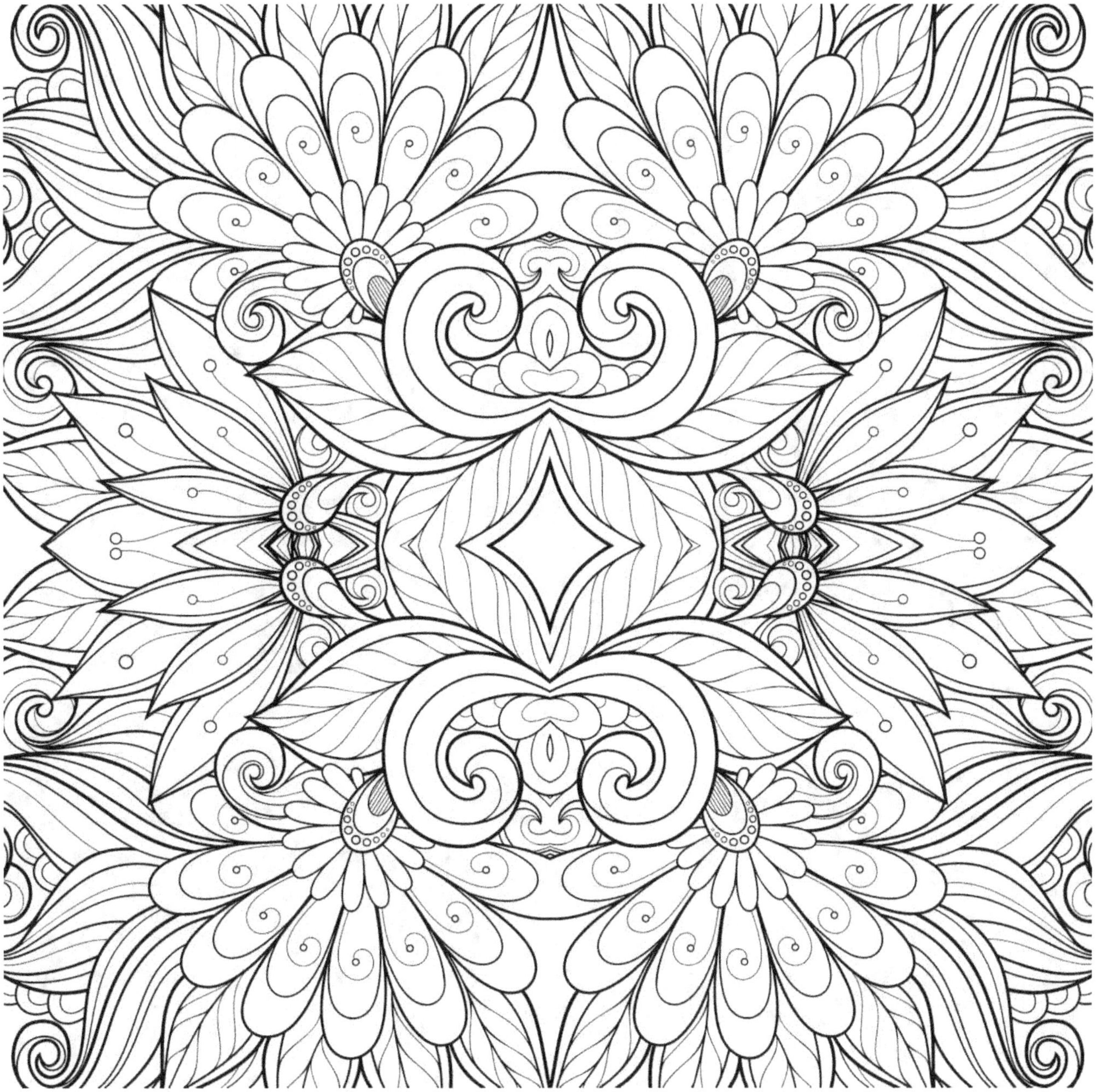

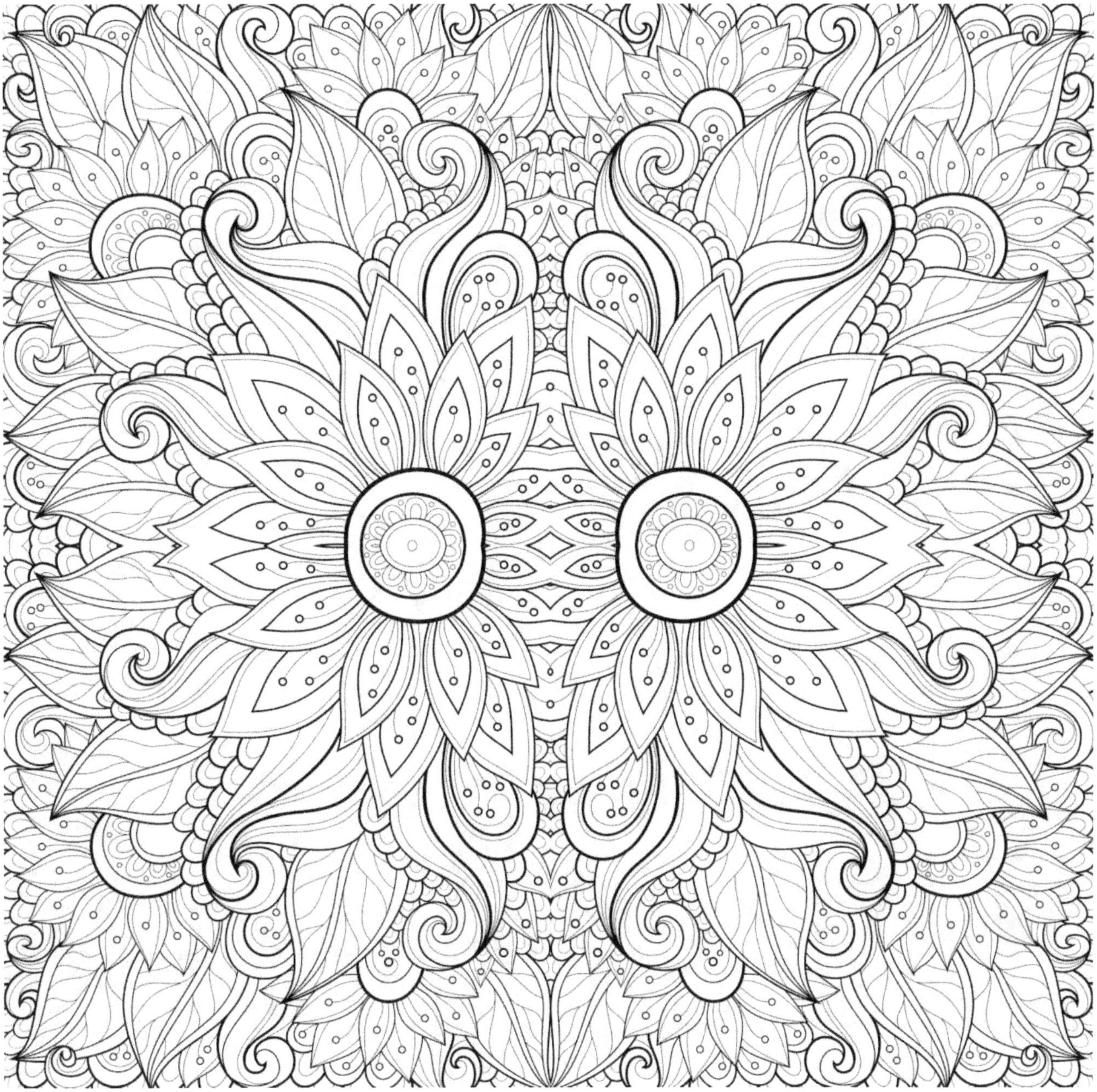

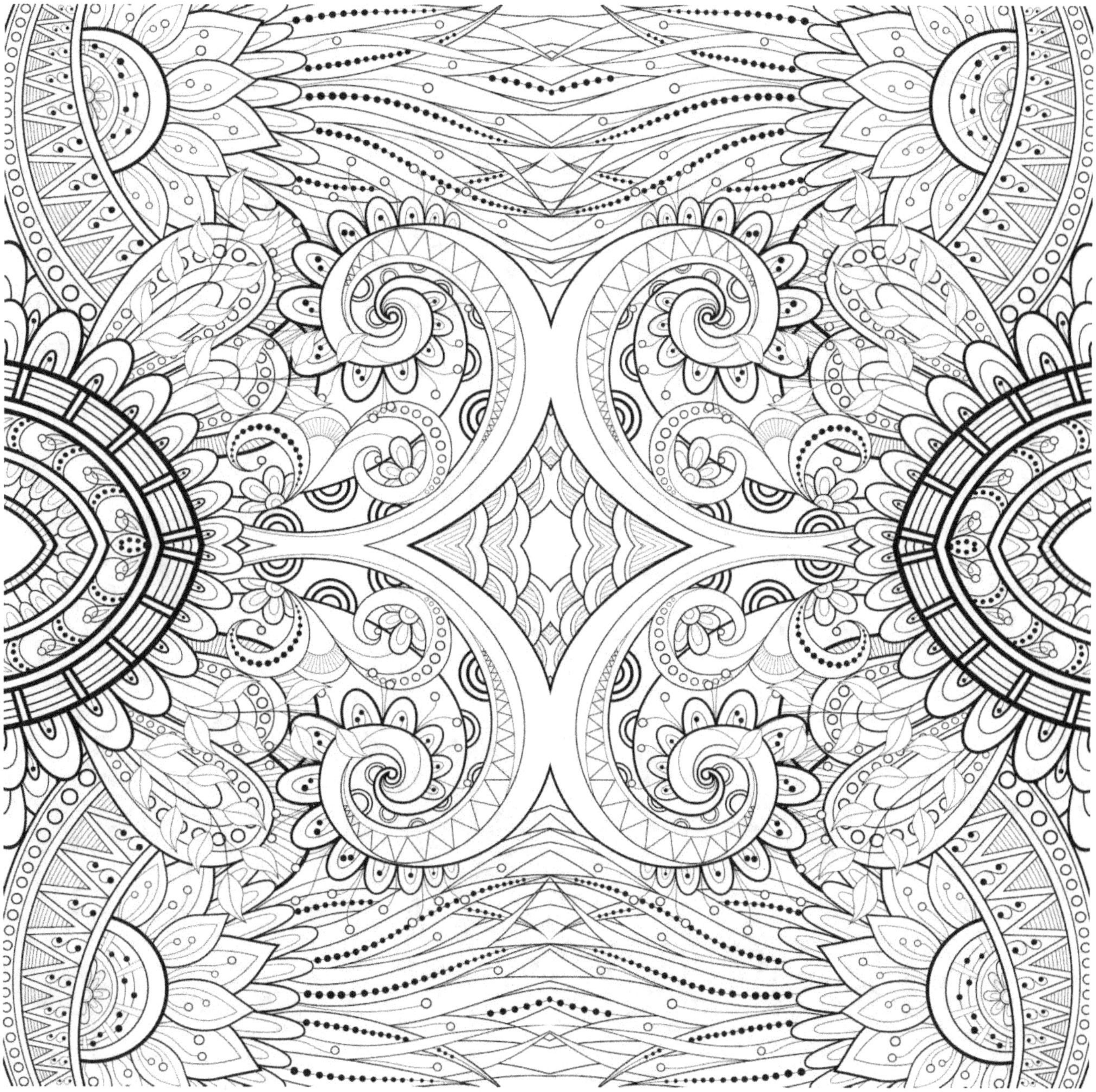

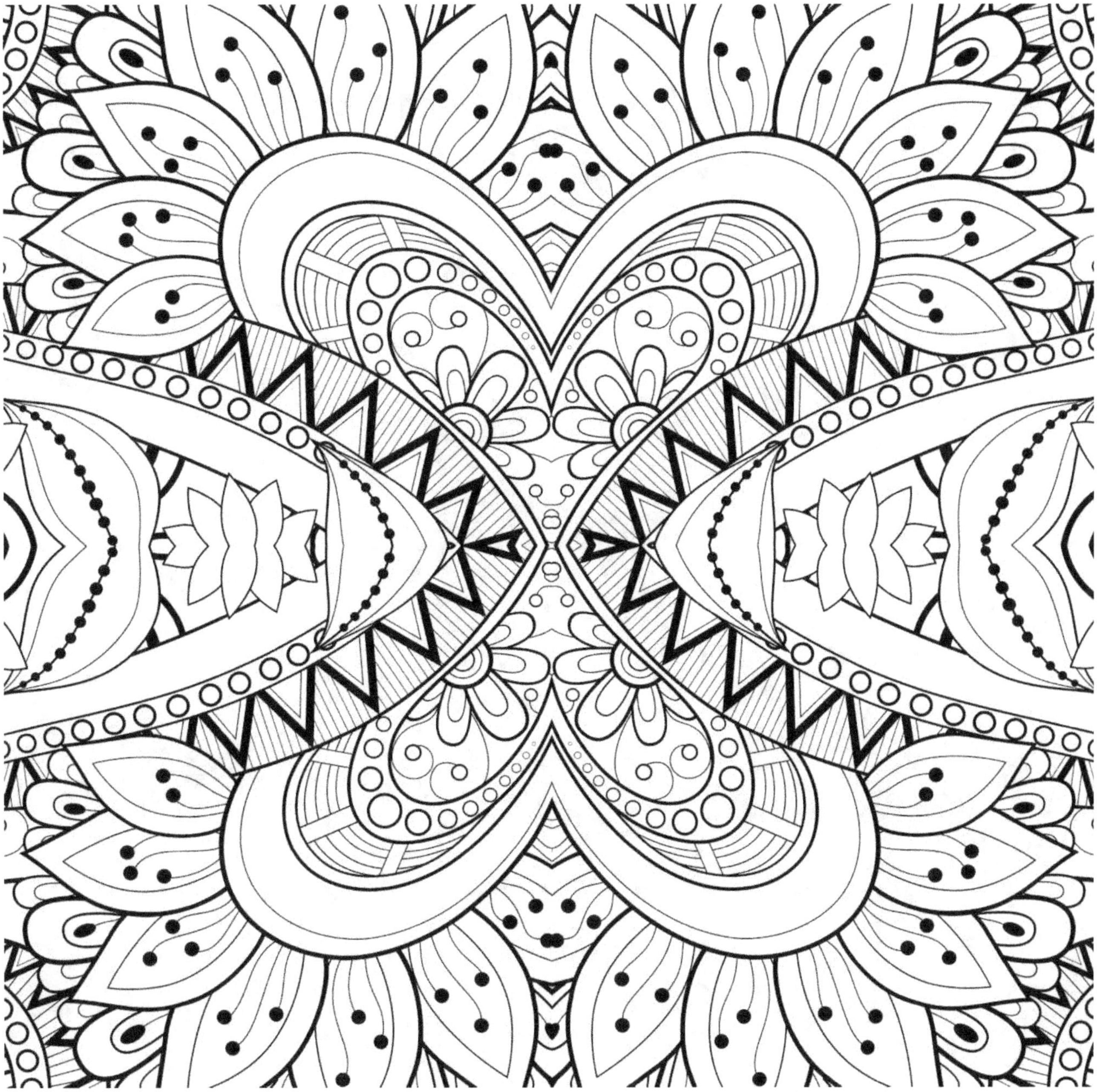

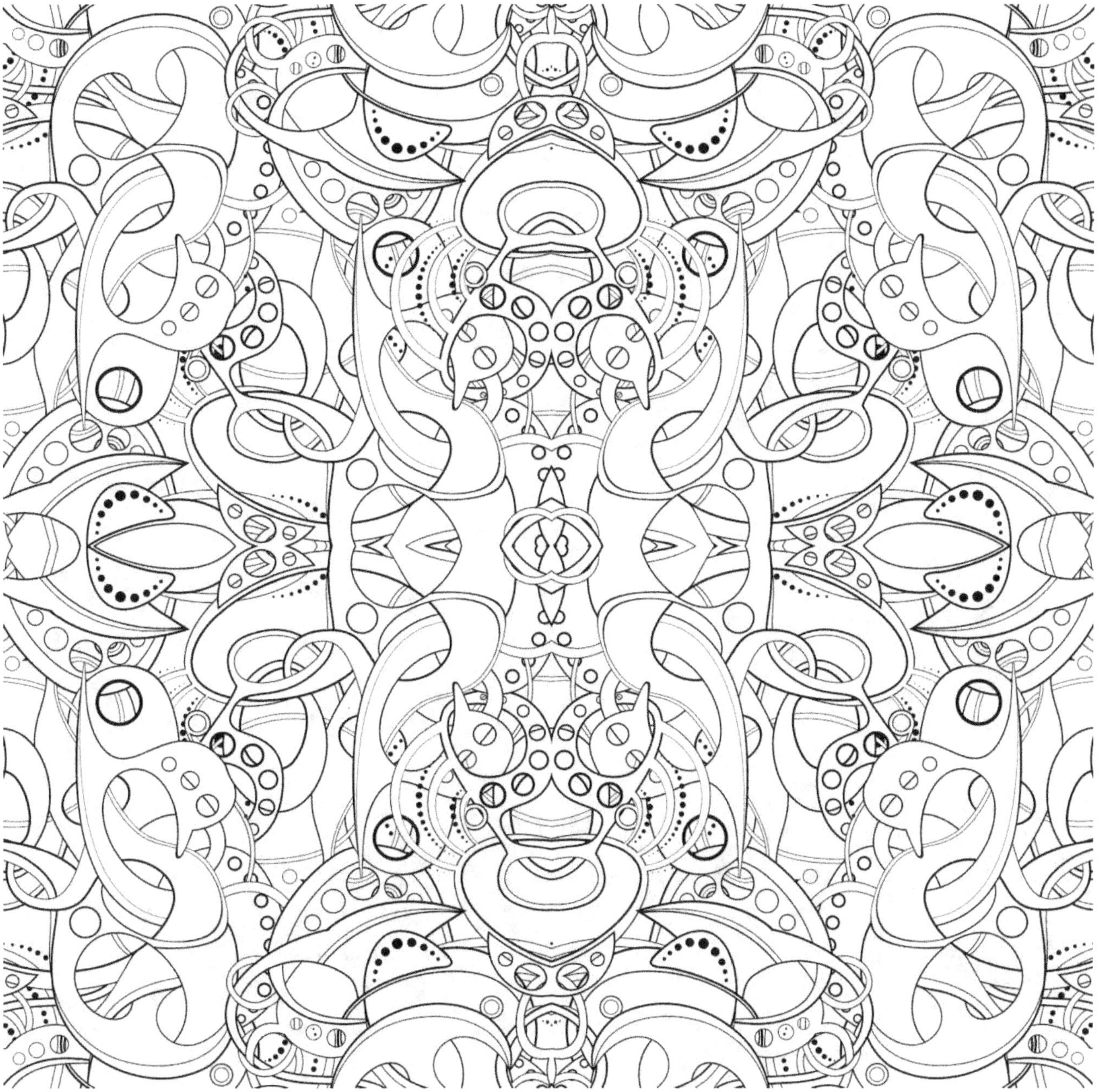

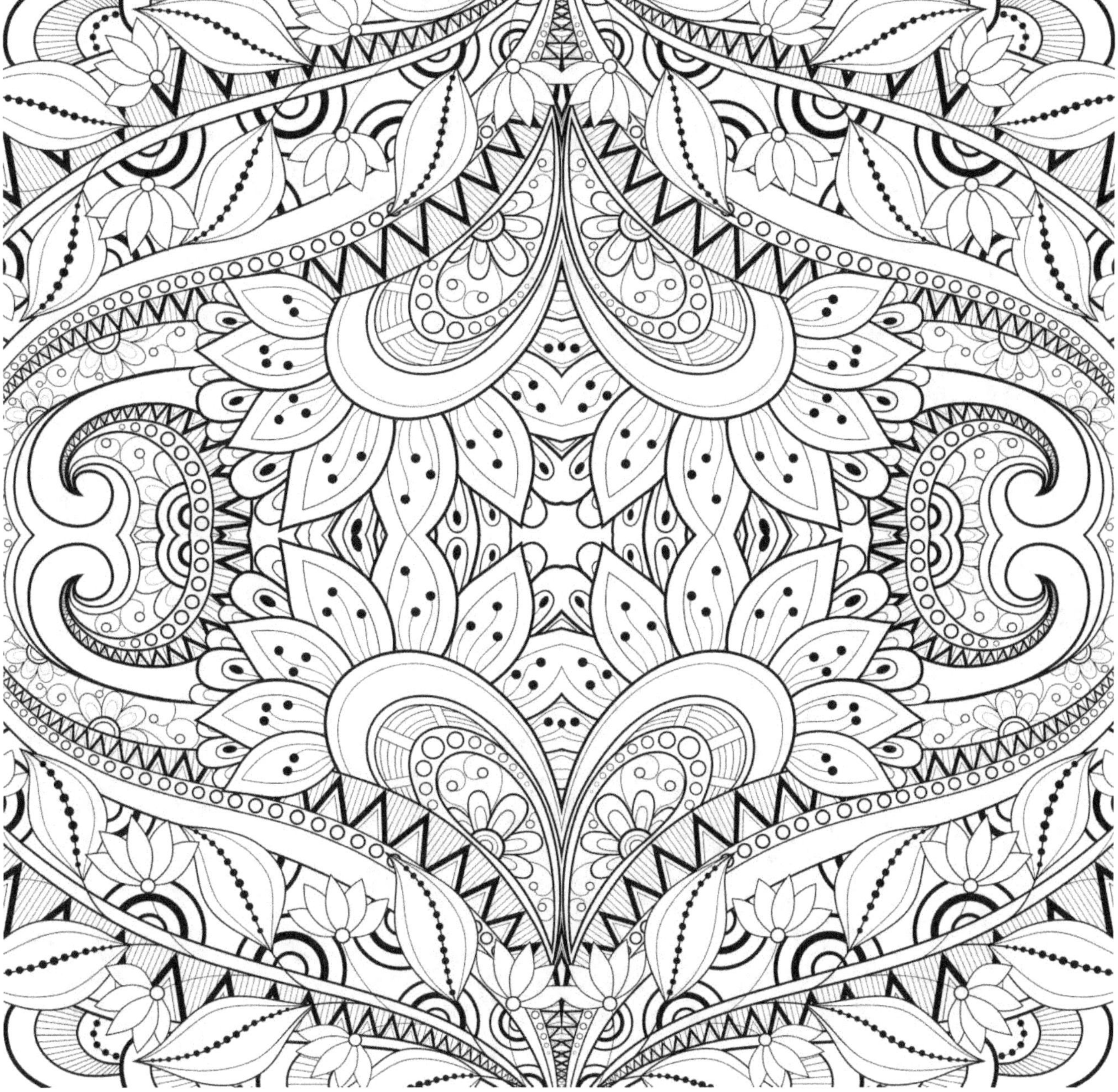

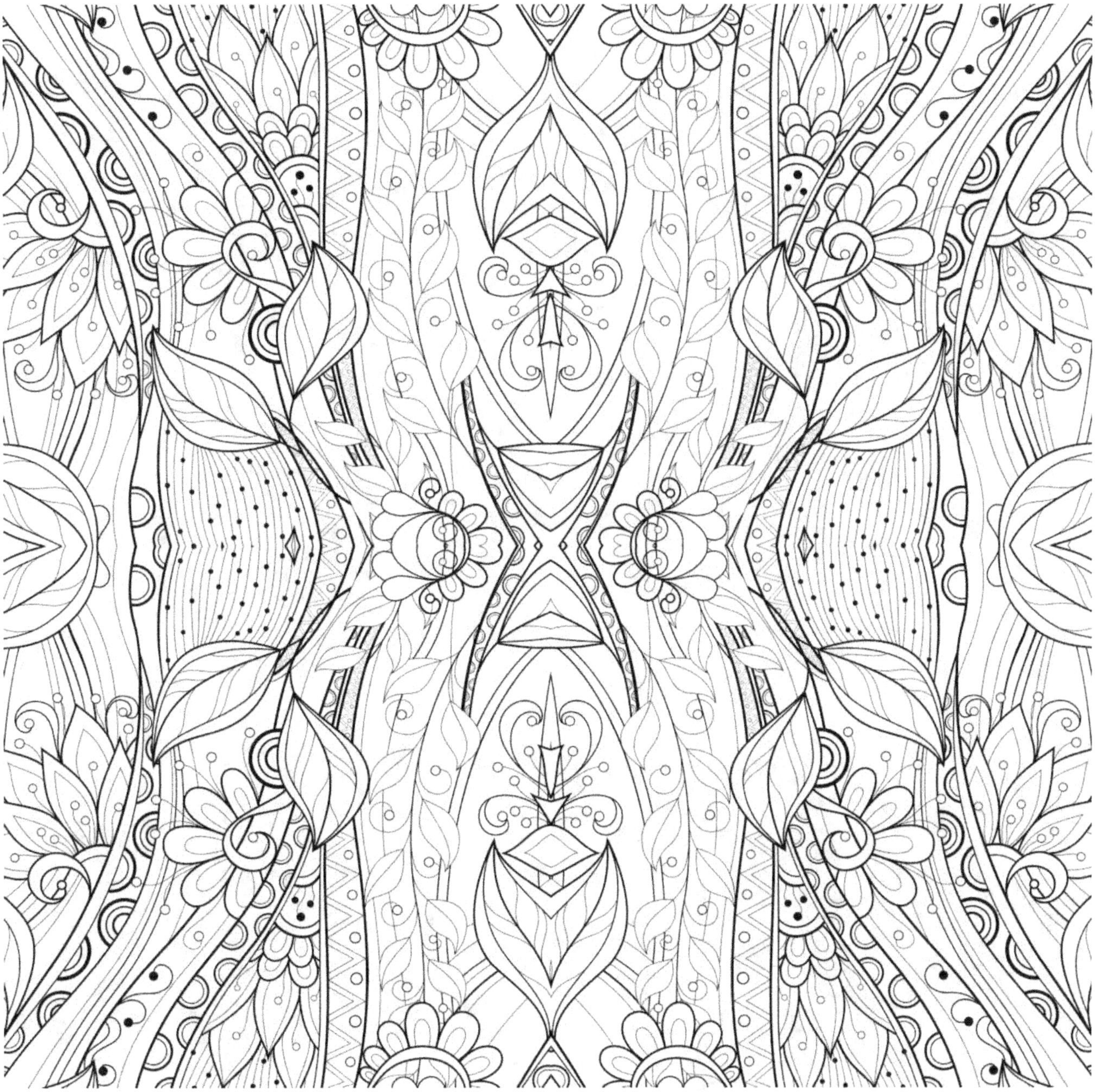

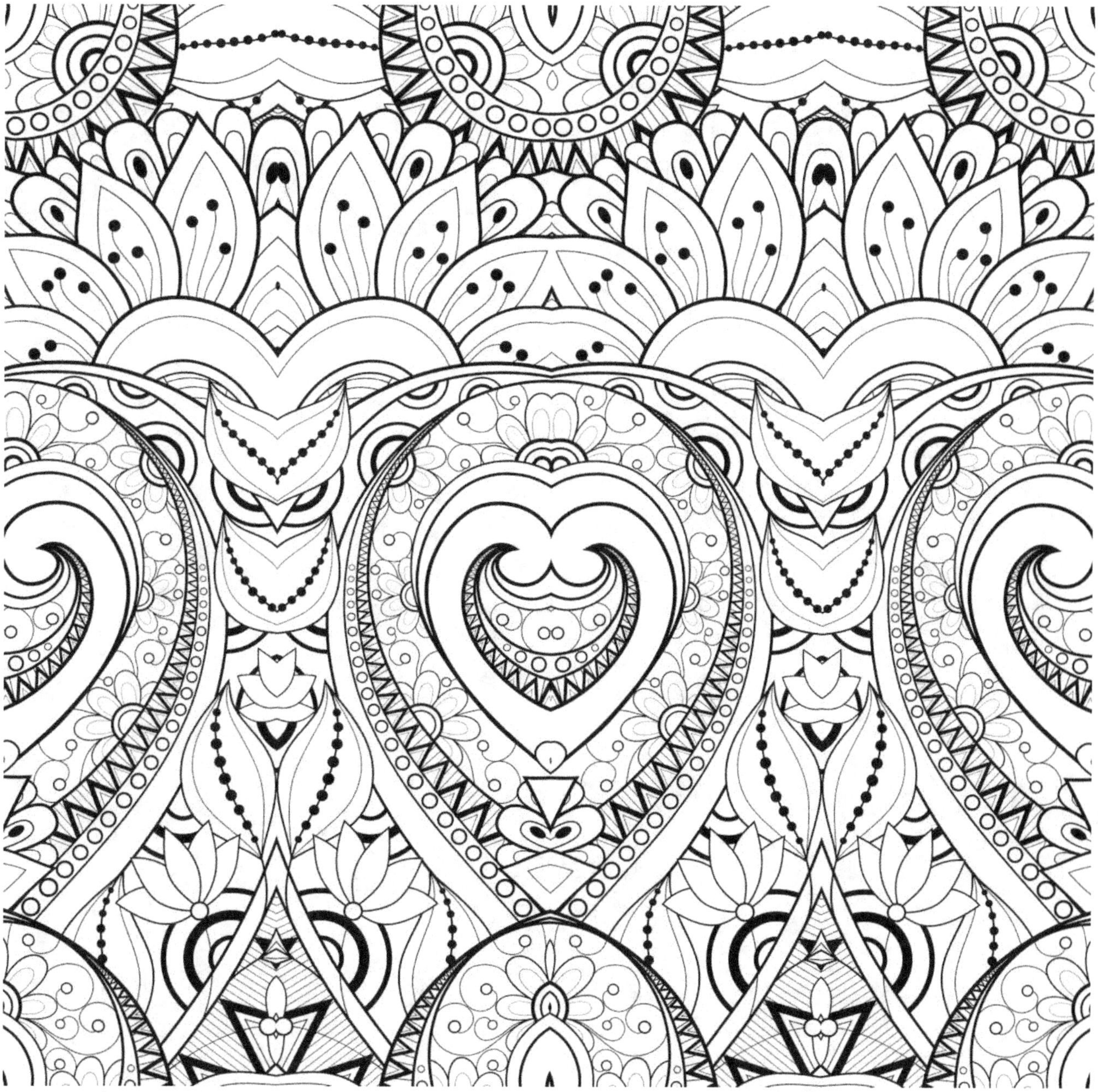

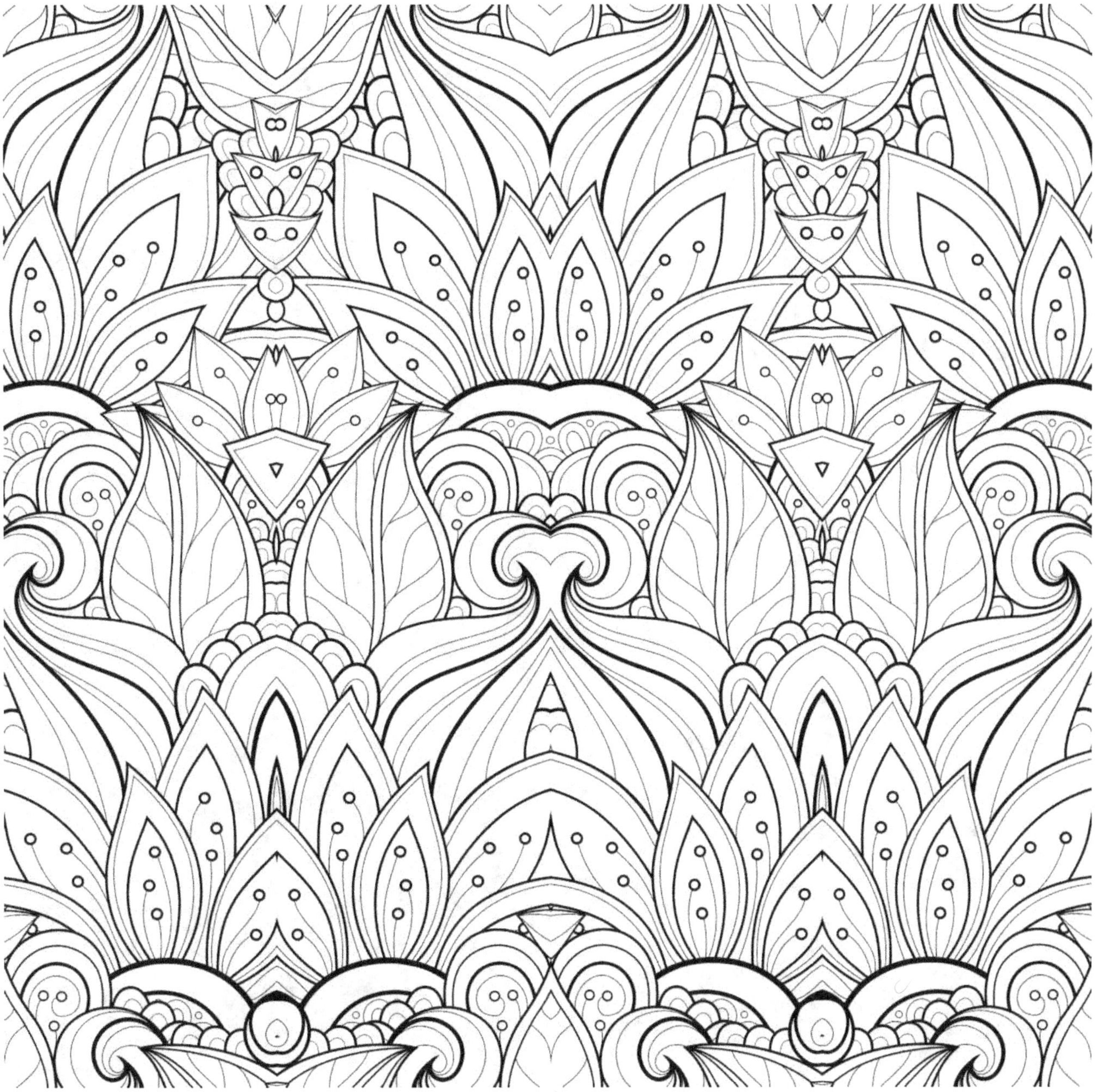

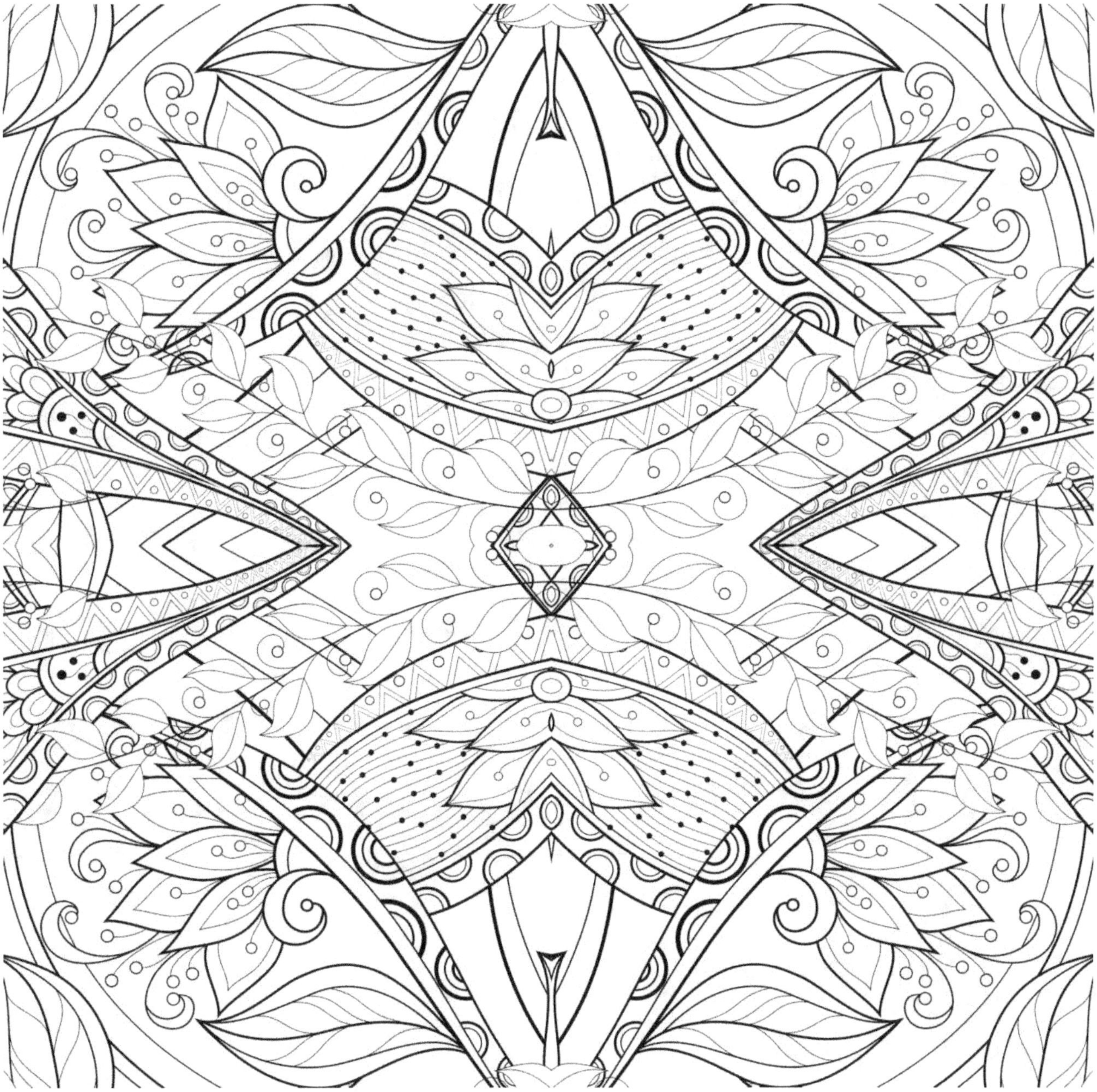

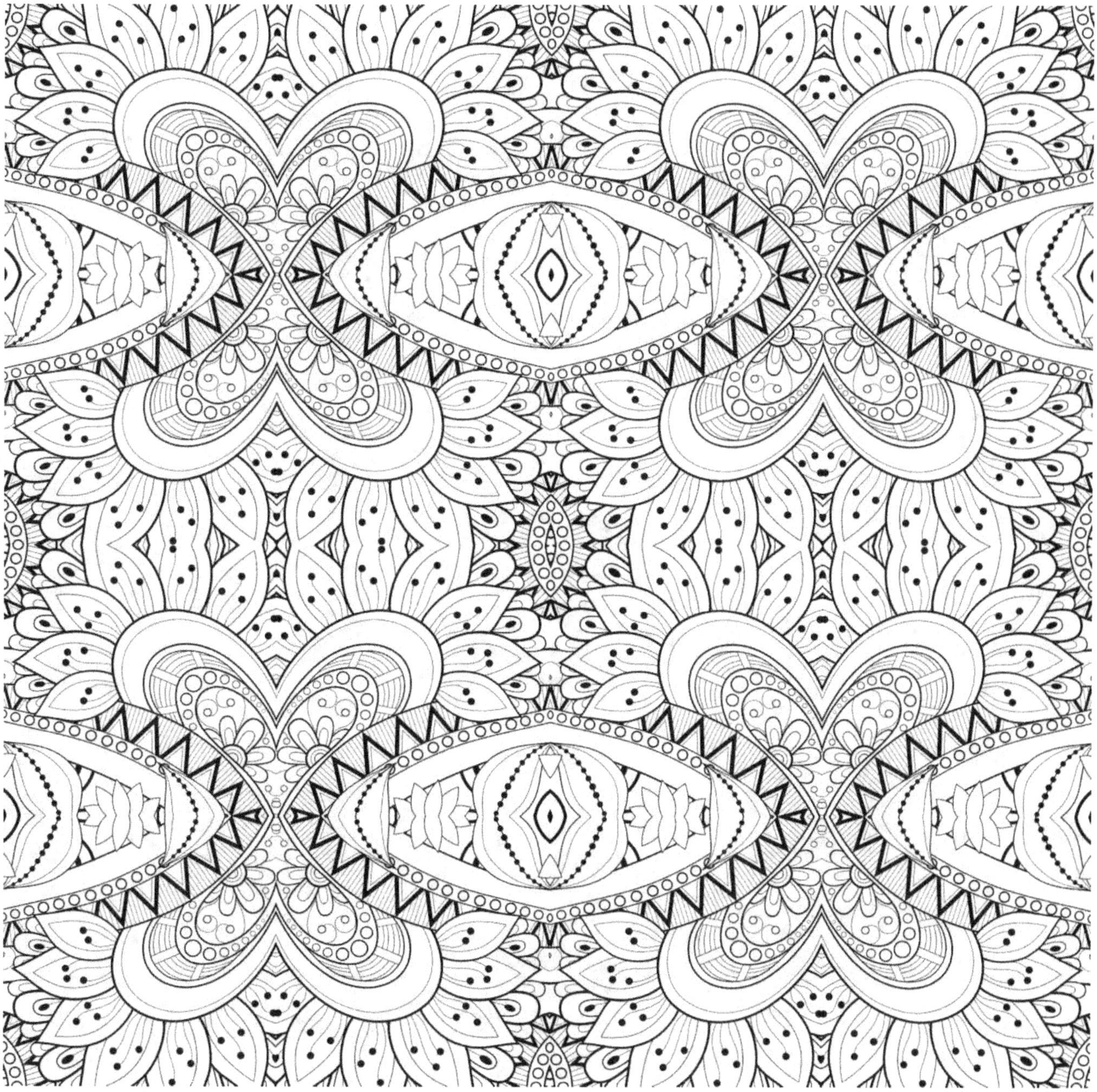

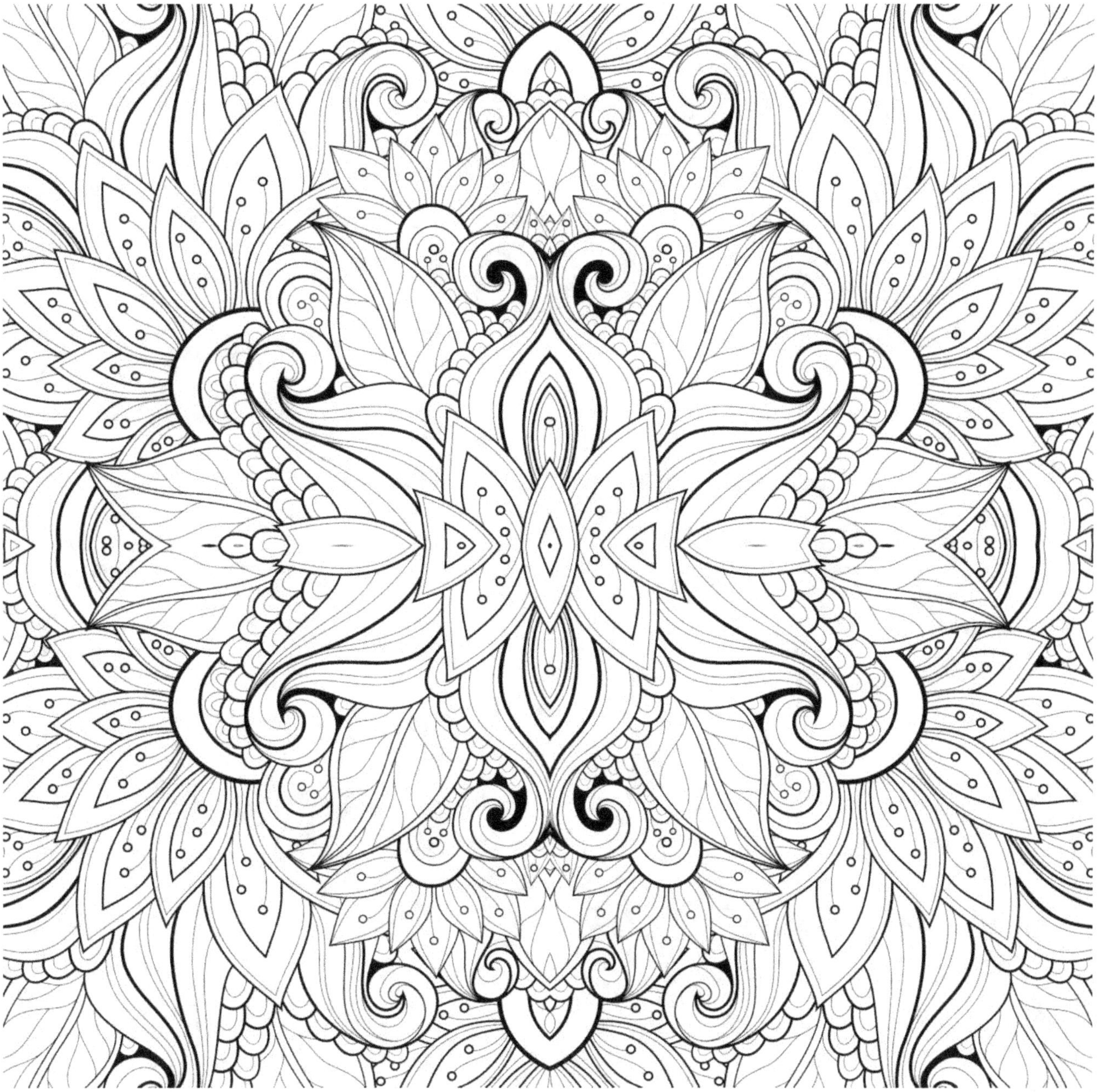

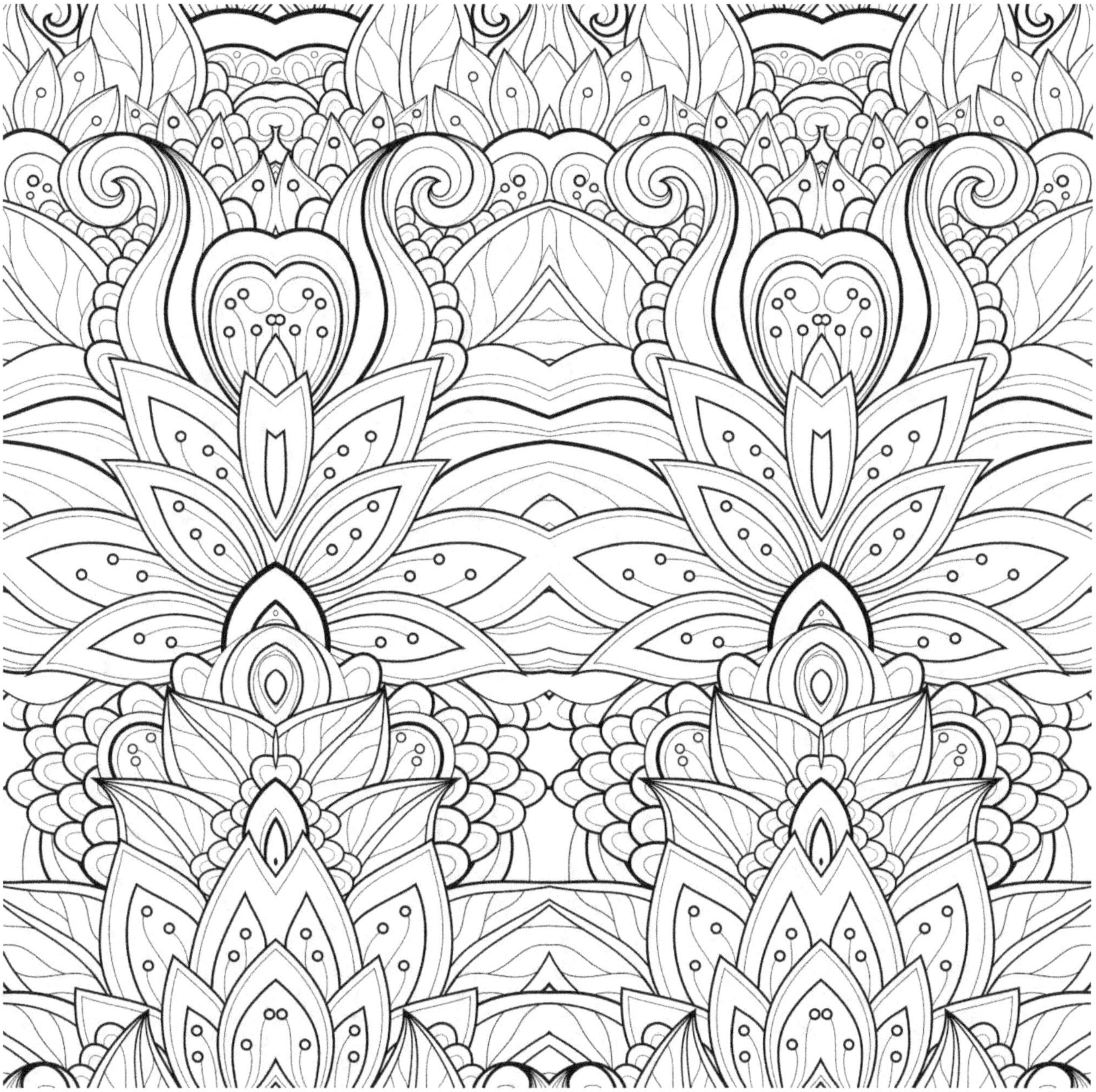

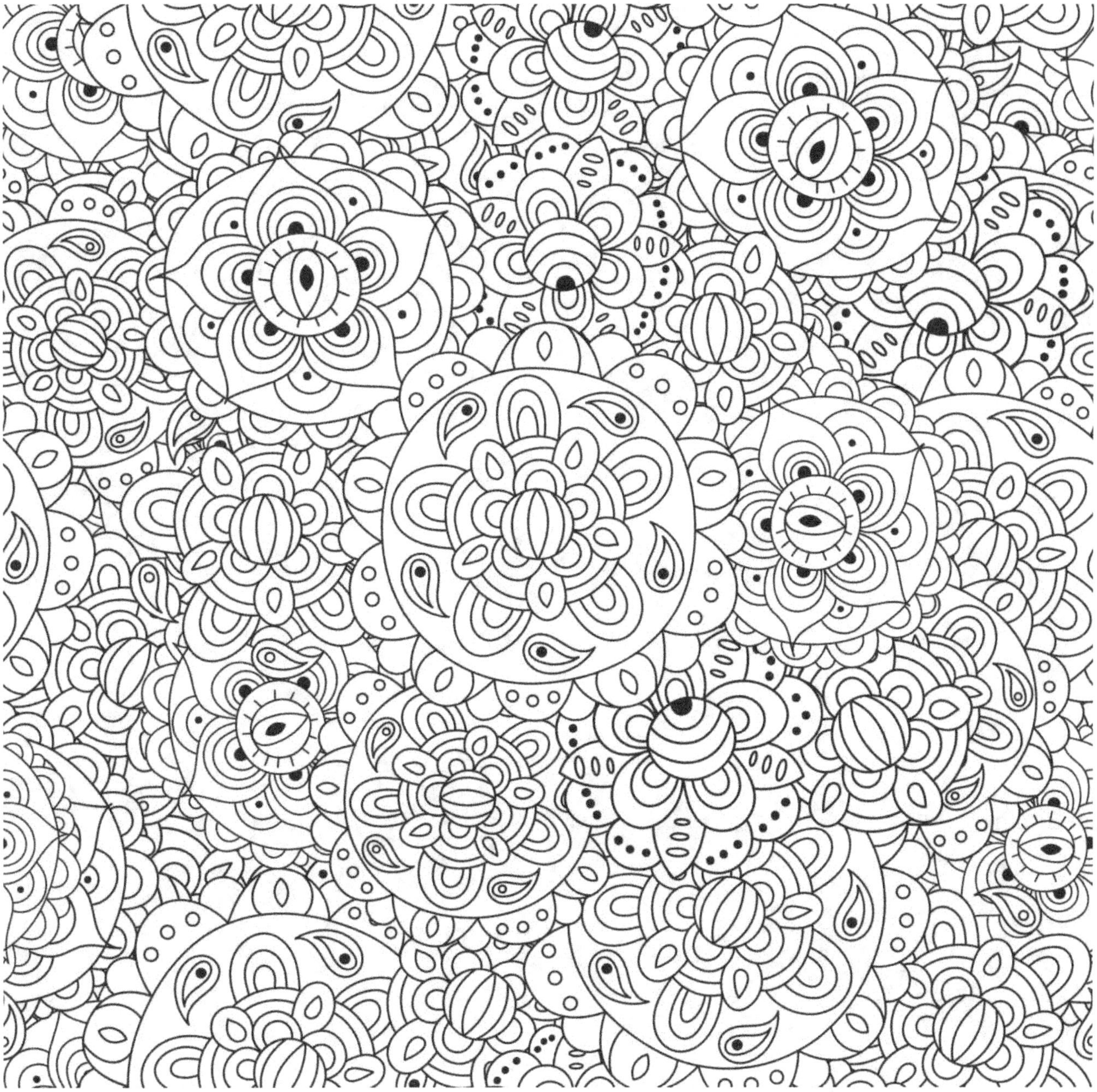

PDF Version of this book : http://bit.ly/seamless_c_2

Don't Miss Another our Books.

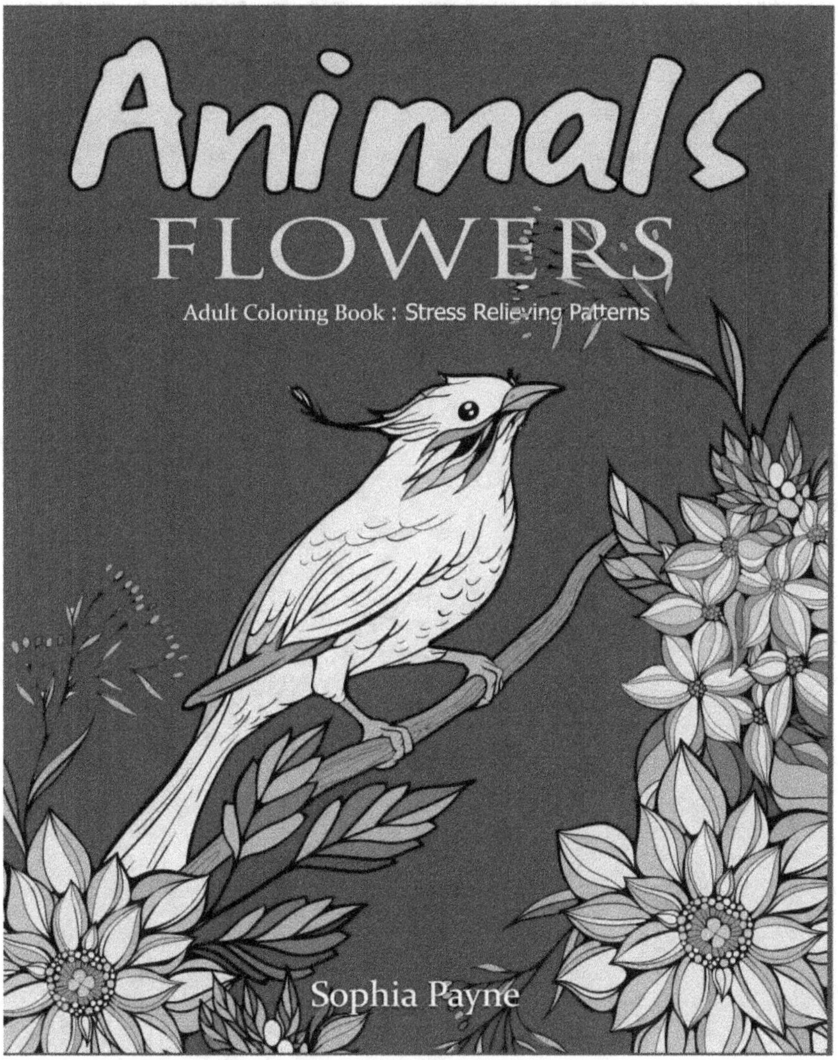

http://bit.ly/animals_flowers_c

ISBN : 9781523987931
(Use this ISBN for searching on amazon.com)

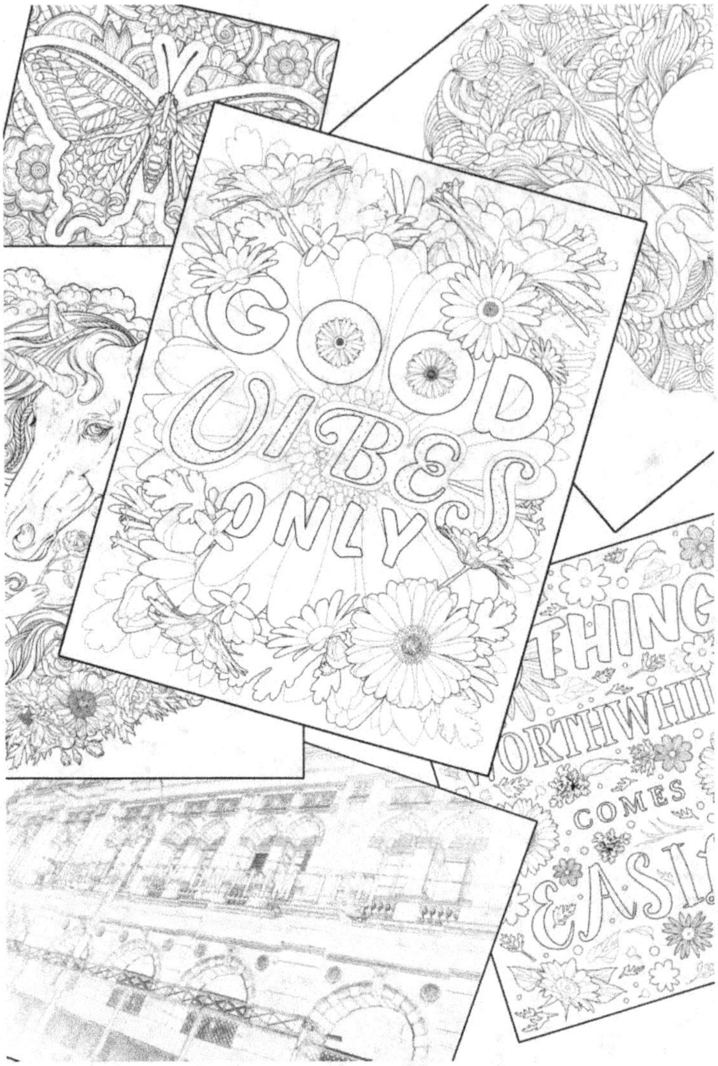
GOOD
VIBES
ONLY
THING
COMES

www.ingramcontent.com/pod-product-compliance
Lightning Source LLC
Chambersburg PA
CBHW081133180526
45170CB00008B/3092
9781540845269